WATER SAFETY

Printed in the United States of America.

Library of Congress Cataloging-in-Publication Data
Loewen, Nancy, 1964-
Water Safety/Nancy Loewen.
p.   cm.
Includes bibliographical references.
Summary: Offers rules for safe behavior while having fun in water.
ISBN 1-56766-261-7   (hard cover : lib. bdg)
1. Swimming for children--Safety measures--Juvenile literature.   2. Aquatic sports-
-Safety measures--Juvenile literature.   [1. Swimming--Safety measures.
2. Aquatic sports--Safety measures.   3. Safety.]
I. Title.
GV838.53.S24L64   1996
797.2'1'083--dc20   95-25885
CIP
AC

WATER SAFETY

By Nancy Loewen Illustrated by Penny Dann

THE CHILD'S WORLD

Swimming, splashing, floating, boating—there are lots of ways to have fun in the water. But playing in the water isn't so much fun if you get hurt, or if you cause someone else to get hurt. That's why it's important to know and follow the safety rules. Pickles and Roy will show you what to do—and what not to do—to stay safe in the water!

Learn how to swim and what to do in an emergency by taking swimming lessons from a **certified** instructor. Practice often so you won't forget.

Swim only when a lifeguard
is present, and stay within
the **designated** swimming
area. Don't swim near boats
or docks.

Know how deep the water is before getting in, especially when jumping or diving.

Always swim with a buddy. That way, if one of you gets into trouble, the other can go for help.

If you feel yourself in danger, try not to panic. Instead, try to float calmly. Help will soon come!

Even if you're a good swimmer, don't overestimate how
far you can swim. The water is no place to take chances!

Never try to rescue a drowning person yourself. If possible, throw a life preserver or any other floating object to the person. Then call for help.

Talk to the lifeguard only when you really need help. Watching over all the people in a pool or at a beach is a serious job, and the lifeguard needs to concentrate.

Obey all the signs that are posted at the pool or beach.

Don't swim on a full stomach. It takes a lot of energy for your body to **digest** a big meal. After eating, wait fifteen minutes before getting into the water.

Watch out for sharp objects in the sand. It's a good idea to wear shoes or sandals when you're not in the water.

Never swim during a thunderstorm. If a thunderstorm comes up while you are swimming, get out of the water right away and seek shelter inside.

Never go into a swimming pool without an adult there to watch you.

Avoid the area under a diving
board. If you're the one diving,
be sure no one is in your way.
Afterwards, be **courteous** and
swim quickly to the side.

Only go into deep water if you're confident of your swimming skills. Floating water toys aren't a substitute for knowing how to swim.

Stay away from unsupervised areas such as **quarries** or **drainage ditches**. The water may contain harmful chemicals or dangerous **debris**.

Always wear a life jacket when you're in a boat. The life jacket should fit snugly and be approved by the U.S. Coast Guard.

Bring an adult with you when you go out in a boat. Stay seated while you're in the boat. If it **capsizes**, stay with the boat until help comes.

Remember these water safety rules every time you're at the pool or beach, and remind your friends to follow the rules, too. The water's great—if you're safe!

23

Glossary

capsizes (CAP-size-is)
to overturn. If your boat capsizes, stay with the boat until help comes.

certified (SIR-ti-fyd)
being true or meeting a standard. Learn how to swim by taking swimming lessons from a certified instructor.

courteous (KUR-te-us)
thoughtful toward others. Be courteous when swimming.

debris (DUH-bree)
the remains of something broken down or destroyed. Water in quarries may contain dangerous debris.

designated (DEZ-ig-nate-ed)
set apart for a specific purpose. When swimming, stay within the designated swimming area.

digest (die-JEST)
to soften and break down by chemicals in the body. It takes a lot of energy for your body to digest a big meal.

drainage (DRANE-ige)
the act of emptying water from one location to another. When there is too much water it may drain into a drainage ditch.

quarries (QUOR-rees)
an open site in the ground used for obtaining stones for building. Stay away from unsupervised areas like quarries.